~101~
MONEY
TIPS
FOR
KIDS
&
PARENTS

This book is dedicated to my mother Jean who inspires me daily with her strength and perseverance. She never gives up.

I also want to thank several people who inspired and encouraged me while creating SKSP (SmartKids SmartParents) and this book: Andrei, Arlene, Carolyn, Joanna, Nelson, Rick, Shirley and Alf.

— F.C.

Published by CBA Productions Ltd.
skspmoneytips@gmail.com
1-877-531-5773
www.sk-sp.com

Designed by Nelson Agustin

ISBN 978-0-9937785-0-6

SMART KIDS ★ SMART PARENTS™

101
MONEY
TIPS

FOR

KIDS
&
PARENTS

FRAN CHRISTIE

INTRODUCTION

The idea for *101 Money Tips for Kids & Parents* was born out of the realization that the times are definitely changing faster than previous generations could have ever imagined. Technology, the internet, social media, and high speed everything is connecting us globally but causing serious disconnect personally; especially with money and how we handle it.

Current statistics confirm the highest rates for bankruptcies, soaring debt, and poverty. Yet there are many people who not only survive but flourish through the financial roller coaster rides so prevalent today. How? From the fundamental money basics they learned, to which we can refer.

101 Money Tips for Kids and Parents is here to teach and remind us to get back to the basics about money. It is for our kids and the kid still in us.

KIDS' BASICS

These basic tips for young kids seem like they are from a by-gone era and yet they are the foundation for a good financial future. Money is more than a swipe of a card, numbers on paper, and does not just magically come out of a machine!

1

Let the kids touch, feel, and learn about real money.

Coins and bills are real and have value. It is vitally important for kids to learn the different denominations, how to make change, and connect money with goods and services.

2

Incorporate an allowance in exchange for chores around the house.

*Teach kids the value of work
in exchange for money
to inspire good work ethics.
Renegotiate as they grow.
Something as simple as putting
their toys away daily can be rewarded
with a quarter or dollar bill as part
of their weekly allowance.*

3
Set goals.

*Teach your kids how much they need to
save if they want to purchase something.
Help them understand the costs
and how they can use their allowance
to pay towards it.*

4
Keep money jars or piggy banks.

*Have the kids label them "Savings",
"Spending", "Giving" or "Education".*

5
Pay their allowance in cash.

*Let them put a portion of their allowance
in each of their special money jars.*

6

Teach kids about banking.

*Do some old-fashioned banking
with your kids. Take them to
a local banking institution and
open a savings account.
Let them do the deposits
(from their money jars).
Do this regularly. This will help them
understand that money does not just
come out of an ATM machine.*

7
Celebrate savings
with the kids.

*Saving money is an accomplishment!
By celebrating it with them,
you will create positive reinforcement
associated with saving.
This simple step will carry them
into adulthood.*

YOUNG ADULTS

Now the basics of basics have been established. The following tips for young adults (teens) are designed to strengthen their relationship to money and to themselves. Goal-setting, saving, negotiating, earning, and costs associated with spending are all part of connecting with money and how to utilize it.

8
Surround yourself
with successful mentors.

They can be family, spiritual, educational business or financial mentors.

9
Plan and prepare for your
post-secondary education.

*There are so many more options in
education than ever before.
Discover what you love to do,
get a certificate or degree
and make a difference for yourself.*

10
Negotiate what jobs/chores will pay you how much.

*This establishes a time/money equation.
Your time is valuable and is worth money.
Determine how much your time is worth
by the quality of work you do.
Good quality work creates
a demand for your time. The greater the
demand the more value it has.*

11
If you have a part-time job, know what benefits/incentives are offered.

Medical, dental, shared profits or tips.

12
Strive for excellence
in all that you do.

Be on time and pay attention.
You will attract more opportunity.

13
Become good at math.

Learn how to calculate percentages,
interest rates, and compound interest.
It is the pathway to financial success.

14
Be respectful to people, kids, animals, and with your "stuff".

How you treat adults, other kids, and your belongings is reflective of how you treat yourself and shows your level of self-esteem. Have respect for you.

15
Understand the Law of Attraction.

The law of attraction is a term given to the belief that "like attracts like" and that, by focusing on positive or negative thoughts, one brings about positive or negative results.

16

Understand the
Law of Reciprocity.

When you do something positive, you will receive a similar response in return. This positive exchange works best when you do things not expecting anything in return. The idea of "pay it forward" is a good example.

17
Be aware of advertising and its influence.

Be conscious of how it influences your decisions about what you purchase.

18
Be aware of peer pressure.

Observe how your friends can influence your decisions around money, education, and your future. Be a good influence on them.

19

Avoid borrowing money— especially from friends or family.

If you do borrow, establish a payment schedule and stick to it until the debt is paid, especially with family and friends.

20
Start a small home-based business to earn money.

Learn to think like an entrepreneur. Create a small business like seasonal lawn maintenance, car washing/detailing, or household maintenance for family, neighbors, and friends.

21
Recycle/Re-sell.

Take good care of what you own now. Well-kept or maintained items like gadgets, sports equipment, electronics, and old toys can have more value when they are in good shape. You can re-sell on eBay or craigslist and make money or trade for something of equal or better value.

22

Shop at garage sales
or thrift stores.

Find great deals and re-sell online or have your own garage sales. This teaches buying and selling, supply and demand, cost and profit margins, marketing and customer service.

23
Establish a long-term savings account

*Put 10% of your paycheck,
any tips you earn, or money that is
gifted to you in a savings account
that you cannot access until
you are at least 18.*

24
Give to charity.

*Donate money or volunteer your time
and skills. This is called "giving back".*

25

Learn financial terms and ask financial questions.

Finances need not be complicated, but it would still be great to learn financial terms as they relate to your investment of time and your money. Start asking: What is the return on my investment of time? Rate of Return (hourly wage)? Profit Margin (How much of my paycheck do I keep)?

26

Learn the pros and cons of credit cards, interest rates, and credit scores before you get one.

27
Be the kid that understands money.

Know how to earn it, save it and how to "make it work for you".

28
Learn the art of negotiating.

Negotiation is a dialogue between two or more people or parties with the intention of reaching an understanding, resolving points of difference, gaining advantage for an individual or collective, or crafting outcomes to satisfy various interests.

Your negotiation skills should always be aimed for the good of all.

29

Understand that money is not about the things you can buy but the freedom it gives.

30

Be a good role model to someone younger than you.

31

Be honest in all your money transactions.

32

Have the courage to save your money.

Save consistently.

33
Learn how to "crunch the numbers".

Incoming money (income) minus outgoing money (expenses) equals what you have left for what you want to do. Money for what you want to do plus working and saving = SUCCESS.

34
Honor and respect your parents.

....and your teachers, police officers, military personnel, employers, and spiritual leaders.

PARENTS
& ADULTS

Having a strong financial foundation is like building a home that can withstand all the elements of nature. The stronger your home and financial foundation, the better you can withstand global and economic elements over which you don't have control. What you can have control over is you and how you use money.

35
Determine your family financial situation right now.

Figure out your household and personal economy. Know how much income is coming in and how much money is spent on expenses. This reflects your financial landscape.

36

Know the operating cost of your household.

Determine what the fixed expenses are versus variable expenses.
Fixed expenses cost the same every month, i.e. mortgage, rent, car insurance, and life insurance.
Variable expenses change monthly such as groceries, gas, and family entertainment.

37
Set your goals as a family.

Set goals for vacations, family time, new vehicle, college etc. Next, cost it out. What is needed, how much to save, how you are going to do it and by when.

38
Show your children what the monthly and household bills look like.

39
Establish the PLAN.

(Better known as the BUDGET).
This is your personal financial roadmap.

40
Learn how to read
a financial statement.

Find out at www.sec.gov.

41

Protect your most important assets.

Your family, your health, and your home is a good place to start.

42

Budget for insurance.

Include in your monthly budget money for life insurance, home insurance, car and health insurance to protect your most valuable assets.

43
Encourage healthy money conversations in your home.

Instead of saying "We can't afford it," try "Let's see how we can make it happen."

44

Differentiate between good debt and bad debt in your household.

Good debt is a home investment or property; bad debt is buying things on credit, making minimum payments, and paying high interest on them.

45

Focus on eliminating BAD debt.

Start with the smallest amount first and feel the satisfaction of paying it off. Establish a schedule and a deadline for paying off all your debts and stick with it. Don't take on any new debts.

46
Know your credit card interest rates and limits.

Calculate what you are paying in interest rates annually on credit cards. Pay them off. Redirect that money to your family goals.

47

Have one credit card for travelling and emergencies only and set a low limit with low interest rates.

Pay it off immediately every month.

48
Get a prepaid visa card.

They are great for students, travelling, gas, and other small expenses. Watch out for fees and get them reloadable.

49
List the unnecessary expenses in your household.

Expenses such as specialty coffees, take-out food, and impulse purchases can really add up. Try to minimize them or go on an impulse purchase diet.

50
New money habit: pay cash.

Cash is still king and remember to ask for a receipt and check the change given.

51
New savings habit:
fill one money jar at a time
with your kids.

52
Label money jars for family projects.

You can label them for special occasions like "Vacation," "Birthday Parties," "Christmas," or "Celebrations."

53
Establish an emergency fund.

*One month at a time and build
to 6 months.*

54
Know your credit score.

*Find out if you have a good credit record.
www.equifax.com   www.equifax.ca
Protect your credit rating by making
payments on time.*

55

Convert your loose change into silver and gold—literally.

*Quarters and dollar bills add up.
Take notice of currency rates and buy
when silver and gold is low—re-sell
when it is higher or collect them for the
grandkids. Store in a safe place.
Go to www.mint.ca (Canadian Mint)
and www.usmint.gov (U.S. Mint).*

56

Take the kids grocery shopping with you and show them what food costs.

Make a grocery list and stick to it.

57

Let your kids pay for what THEY want out of their savings.

This helps establish needs as opposed to wants and the consequences of their purchase choices. Do they really want that candy bar if they have to pay for it?

58
Avoid shopping at convenience stores.

The prices are higher with more temptations, such as junk food.

59
Have a meal before grocery shopping.

Shopping for groceries on empty stomach costs more money—all discipline goes out the window.

60
Use coupons
wherever possible.

61
Get your younger children to
cut out the coupons with you.

*Buy staple items in bulk or by the case
or with a group of friends or family.*

62
Buy a small to medium size freezer.

63
Support your local Farmers' Market and eat local.

*Healthy nutritious foods are
less expensive in the long run
and healthier.
Grow your own food by planting
vegetables, fruit-bearing plants,
and herbs. Make your own jam, dry or can
your own food for long term storage.*

64
Keep a well-stocked pantry.

Keep the basics on hand like pasta, canned tuna, beans, flour, and spices for quick meals.

65
Exchange toddlers' clothing with other parents.

Create an exchange of gently-used clothing and toys for toddlers.

66
Go treasure hunting at second-hand and thrift stores.

There is always a bargain for gently used kids clothes, household items, appliances, furniture, etc. Often times good quality used stuff is better than the poor quality new stuff. For example, cleaning old appliances or refinishing wood furniture make them look newer. There are some great bargains online as well.

67

Encourage your kids to negotiate their household chores and tasks with you.

See tip # 10.

68

Give your children incentives of raises or bonuses for excellence.

See tip # 12.

69

Keep your promises.
Period.

70

Stand by your word.

"Yes" means "yes" and "no" means "no."
But be willing to renegotiate.

71
Play Monopoly with your kids.

Or other money games where you can learn and have fun as a family.

72
Avoid impulse purchases.

The small ones lead you to the big ones that you may regret.

73
Avoid impulse giving.

See tip # 72.

74
Your kids watch how you manage and spend your money.

They will do the same.

75
Practice delayed gratification.

*"Let me think about it," is a good standard
response then walk away. This works.*

76

Discuss the cost and responsibilities of having pets with your kids.

Help them understand the cost of pet food and vet bills, and who is responsible for them. By helping to contribute to the cost and care of their pet, they learn a good first lesson about long-term responsibility.

77

Calculate the cost to be involved in sports/ dance/ extra school activities.

Then add 15% to the budget to allow for any unexpected expenses.

78

Establish a small family home-based business.

This encourages entrepreneurship, work ethic, teamwork, and business savvy.

79
Ask for a receipt for all purchases.

Save your receipts for one month and calculate what you spent. Determine where you can save.

80
Sort receipts by category.

You can separate them for food, gas, school supplies, etc. Get the kids to help. This establishes good practice in monitoring monthly money expenditures.

81
Retail therapy only provides temporary relief.

Don't window-shop, go to the mall or shop online while upset, stressed or emotional.

82
Stay away from infomercials late at night.

Take advice from tip # 81.

83
Manage your spending fix.

*If you need a spending fix,
go to a dollar store or a thrift store.
The brain does not differentiate between
a $1.00 item and a $100.00 item.
It just needs to go through the process.*

84
Pay your cell phone bill on time and avoid late charges or cancellation.

*Check with your cell phone provider
every 3 months to negotiate
a better rate or package.*

85
Calculate your annual cable bill.

Figure out the value of having cable versus what you could do with the money you save by canceling it. Do you think you would have more family time, vacation time, etc.? Renegotiate the cable bill every 3 months if you want to keep it. (Netflix is a good alternative for considerably less cost and no commercials.)

86
Avoid signing a long term contract with a cell phone company or cable company.

Prepaid or pay-as-you-go cell phones are great. Read the fine print on any contract you need to sign.

87
Encourage reading and intellectual pursuits with your kids instead of TV.

The local library is still a great resource for learning, family activity and local community announcements.

88

Encourage your kids to have a part-time job after the age of 16.

Then help them manage the money they earn.

89

Pay attention to small charges that add up to unnecessary expenditures.

Expenses like bank charges, interest rates, fees, penalties, and contracts can add up!

90
When purchasing a car, factor in ALL expenses.

Whether the car is new or used, determine all expenses like payments, interest rates, car insurance, and gas. Read the contract before you sign it. Ask questions and take your time. Get references for a reputable car dealer. Clarify. Don't feel pressured.

91

Be diligent about filing and paying taxes on time.

This saves you potential penalties and interest, and this also gives you peace from "the taxman".

92
Be an informed consumer.

Do your research regarding products and services that pertain to you and your household. Check out www.consumerreports.org.

93

New shopping habit: question every purchase and every expense.

Do I really need it? Do I just want it?

94
Be diligent in paying your credit card balance.

Paying the credit card balance every month potentially saves hundreds of dollars in interest annually. That is more money in your pocket.

95

There is a difference between being cheap and being frugal.

Frugal is good. Cheap is less favorable. Frugality is a quality of being prudent and not wasteful. Cheap suggests that you are not willing to pay for anything.

96

Establish your financial goals before choosing a financial advisor.

Choose an advisor that will work with you.

97

Learn financial terminology with your family.

Do some online research and have someone like a financial advisor explain financial terms with you and your family.

98
Establish a circle of support.

Get referrals for services like household, financial planning, banking, etc. Ask for references.

99
Barter.

*Try to do an exchange of services
or items of similar value.
Be creative! Have fun!*

100
Prepare a will.

This is important especially if you are the main wage earner and have children. Regardless if you are single, separated or divorced, have a will.

101
Give thanks for something new each day.

This builds an attitude of gratitude.

ABOUT THE AUTHOR

Fran Christie has worked in a sales and marketing capacity in a variety of industries with over 30 years experience. In the course of her career, she has found a common theme when discussing financial matters with friends, clients, and for herself: very few of us were taught fundamental money principles growing up, either from our family or in school. She feels that an informed conversation about money is vitally important anytime in life but the ideal is to start at an early age.

Aside from discussing current day topics such as finance, Fran enjoys being with people, the outdoors, fitness, sailing, horseback riding and a healthy lifestyle. She believes that kids are the future, families are the strength of society and seniors are to be honored and live in dignity.

Fran lives in a beautiful seaside community in Vancouver, Canada.